smoothies
and juices

simple and delicious easy-to-make recipes

Christine Ambridge

This is a Parragon Book
This edition published in 2003

Parragon
Queen Street House
4 Queen Street
Bath
BA1 1HE, UK

Hardback ISBN: 1-40542-097-9
Paperback ISBN: 1-40542-098-7

Printed in China

Produced by the Bridgewater Book Company Ltd.

Photographer Calvey Taylor-Haw

Home Economist Michaela Taylor-Haw

NOTES FOR THE READER

• This book uses both metric and imperial
measurements. Follow the same units of
measurement throughout; do not mix metric
and imperial.

• All spoon measurements are level: teaspoons
are assumed to be 5 ml, and tablespoons are
assumed to be 15 ml.

• Unless otherwise stated, milk is assumed to
be full fat, eggs and individual vegetables such
as carrots are medium, and pepper is freshly
ground black pepper.

• Recipes using raw eggs should be avoided
by infants, the elderly, pregnant women,
convalescents, and anyone suffering from
an illness.

• The times given are an approximate guide
only. Preparation times differ according to
the techniques used by different people and
the cooking times may also vary from those
given. Optional ingredients, variations or
serving suggestions have not been included
in the calculations.

contents

introduction

There has never been a better time to enjoy the wonderful benefits of smoothies and juices. Our local shops and supermarkets are bursting with tantalising fresh fruits and vegetables, and many of them are in plentiful supply all year round.

You can also enjoy seasonal fruits at any time of year simply by freezing them. Peel them first if necessary, cut into slices or cubes, then arrange them in a single layer on a tray and freeze them. You can then transfer them to freezer bags, ready for use.

The drinks in this book are quick to prepare, easy to digest, and full of vitamins, minerals and other healthy life-enhancing substances. Bananas, for example, are a rich source of potassium and magnesium, and can help lower cholesterol levels. Mangoes are full of vitamin A, which is a powerful cancer-fighting agent. Pineapples contain bromelain, an enzyme that helps ease inflammation and soothes the digestion; and tomatoes contain vitamin E, a valuable antioxidant that helps combat the ageing process.

You can enjoy the drinks in this book at any time of day. Within these pages you will find refreshing morning pick-me-ups, nutritious lunchtime drinks, delicious dinner combinations, and stunning concoctions for entertaining that will have your guests coming back for more. So, whatever the time of day, or whatever the occasion, this book will ensure you have the perfect drink every time.

cinnamon & lemon tea

page 24

watercress float

page 42

pineapple soda

page 70

cherry kiss

page 92

morning refreshers

What better way to wake up than to treat your taste buds to an explosion of mouthwatering flavours? The delicious drinks in this section will uplift your senses and leave you feeling refreshed and ready for whatever the day will bring. Whether your idea of a good breakfast treat is an energising Red Pepper Reactor, a cool Peppermint Ice, or a relaxing and luxurious Pacific Smoothie, there is bound to be something here to tempt you and ensure a perfect start to your day.

melon

medley

how hard ✳ extremely easy

serves ✳ two

prep time ✳ 15 minutes

cooking time ✳ —

ingredients

250 ml/9 fl oz
natural yogurt

100 g/3½ oz
galia melon,
cut into chunks

100 g/3½ oz
cantaloupe melon,
cut into chunks

100 g/3½ oz
watermelon,
cut into chunks

6 ice cubes

to decorate

wedges of
melon

✳ Pour the yogurt into a food processor. Add the galia melon chunks and process until smooth.

✳ Add the cantaloupe and watermelon chunks along with the ice cubes and process until smooth. Pour the mixture into glasses and decorate with wedges of melon. Serve at once.

fruit

cooler

how hard ✳ extremely easy

serves ✳ two

prep time ✳ 10 minutes

cooking time ✳ —

ingredients

250 ml/9 fl oz
orange juice

125 ml/4 fl oz
natural yogurt

2 eggs

2 bananas,
sliced and frozen

to decorate

slices of fresh
banana

✳ Pour the orange juice and yogurt into a food processor and process gently until combined.

✳ Add the eggs and frozen bananas and process until smooth. Pour the mixture into glasses and decorate the rims with slices of fresh banana. Add straws and serve.

pacific
smoothie

how hard ✳ extremely easy
serves ✳ two
prep time ✳ 15 minutes
cooking time ✳ 15 minutes

ingredients

350 ml/12 fl oz
hazelnut yogurt

2 tbsp freshly squeezed
orange juice

4 tbsp
maple syrup

8 large fresh figs,
chopped

6 ice cubes

to decorate

toasted chopped
hazelnuts

✳ Pour the yogurt, orange juice and maple syrup into a food processor and process gently until combined.

✳ Add the figs and ice cubes and process until smooth. Pour the mixture into glasses and scatter over some toasted chopped hazelnuts. Serve at once.

red pepper
reactor

how hard ❈ extremely easy
serves ❈ two
prep time ❈ 15 minutes
cooking time ❈ —

ingredients

250 ml/9 fl oz
carrot juice

250 ml/9 fl oz
tomato juice

2 large red peppers,
deseeded and roughly chopped

1 tbsp
lemon juice

to serve

freshly ground
black pepper

✳ Pour the carrot juice and tomato juice into a food processor and process gently until combined.

✳ Add the red peppers and lemon juice. Season with plenty of freshly ground black pepper and process until smooth. Pour the mixture into tall glasses, add straws and serve.

ginger
crush

how hard ❋ very easy
serves ❋ two
prep time ❋ 15 minutes
cooking time ❋ —

ingredients

250 ml/9 fl oz
carrot juice

4 tomatoes,
skinned, deseeded and
roughly chopped

1 tbsp
lemon juice

25 g/1 oz
fresh parsley

1 tbsp grated
fresh root ginger

6 ice cubes

125 ml/4 fl oz
water

to garnish
chopped fresh **parsley**

❋ Put the carrot juice, tomatoes and lemon juice into a food processor and process gently until combined.

❋ Add the parsley to the food processor along with the ginger and ice cubes. Process until well combined, then pour in the water and process until smooth.

❋ Pour the mixture into tall glasses and garnish with chopped fresh parsley. Serve at once.

cranberry

energiser

how hard ✳ extremely easy

serves ✳ two

prep time ✳ 10 minutes

cooking time ✳ —

ingredients

300 ml/10 fl oz
cranberry juice

100 ml/3½ fl oz
orange juice

150 g/5½ oz
fresh raspberries

1 tbsp
lemon juice

to decorate

slices and spirals
of fresh **lemon**
or **orange**

✳ Pour the cranberry juice and orange juice into a food

processor and process gently until combined. Add the raspberries

and lemon juice and process until smooth.

✳ Pour the mixture into glasses and decorate with slices and

spirals of fresh lemon or orange. Serve at once.

nectarine

melt

how hard ❊ extremely easy

serves ❊ two

prep time ❊ 15 minutes

cooking time ❊ —

ingredients

250 ml/9 fl oz
milk

350 g/12 oz
lemon sorbet

1 ripe mango,
stoned and diced

2 ripe nectarines,
stoned and diced

❊ Pour the milk into a food processor, add half of the lemon sorbet and process gently until combined. Add the remaining sorbet and process until smooth.

❊ When the mixture is thoroughly blended, gradually add the mango and nectarines and process until smooth. Pour the mixture into glasses, add straws and serve.

peppermint
ice

how hard ✳ extremely easy

serves ✳ two

prep time ✳ 10 minutes

cooking time ✳ —

ingredients

150 ml/5 fl oz
milk

2 tbsp
peppermint syrup

400 g/14 oz
peppermint ice cream

to decorate

sprigs of fresh **mint**

✳ Pour the milk and peppermint syrup into a food processor and process gently until combined.

✳ Add the peppermint ice cream and process until smooth. Pour the mixture into tall glasses and decorate with sprigs of fresh mint. Add straws and serve.

cinnamon & lemon

tea

how hard ✳ extremely easy

serves ✳ two

prep time ✳ 8–10 minutes

cooking time ✳ 3–4 minutes

ingredients

400 ml/14 fl oz
water

4 cloves

1 small stick of
cinnamon

2 tea bags

3–4 tbsp
lemon juice

1–2 tbsp
brown sugar

to decorate

slices of fresh **lemon**

✳ Put the water, cloves and cinnamon into a saucepan and bring to the boil. Remove from the heat and add the tea bags. Leave to infuse for 5 minutes, then remove the tea bags.

✳ Stir in lemon juice and sugar to taste. Return the pan to the heat and warm through gently.

✳ Remove the pan from the heat and strain the tea into heatproof glasses. Decorate with slices of fresh lemon and serve.

orange & lime iced

tea

how hard ✳ very easy

serves ✳ two

prep time ✳ 15 minutes
+ 1¼ hours to chill

cooking time ✳ 3–4 minutes

ingredients

300 ml/10 fl oz
water

2 tea bags

100 ml/3½ fl oz
orange juice

4 tbsp
lime juice

1–2 tbsp
brown sugar

8 ice cubes

to decorate

wedge of **lime**

granulated **sugar**

slices of fresh **orange,
lemon** or **lime**

✳ Pour the water into a saucepan and bring to the boil. Remove from the heat, add the tea bags and leave to infuse for 5 minutes. Remove the tea bags and leave the tea to cool to room temperature (about 30 minutes). Transfer to a jug, cover with clingfilm and chill in the refrigerator for at least 45 minutes.

✳ When the tea has chilled, pour in the orange juice and lime juice. Add sugar to taste.

✳ Take two glasses and rub the rims with a wedge of lime, then dip them in granulated sugar to frost. Put the ice cubes into the glasses and pour over the tea. Decorate the rims with slices of fresh orange, lemon or lime and serve.

Make your lunchtimes special with the delightful drinks on the following pages. They are packed

with life-giving nutrients and use the freshest, most delicious ingredients. Why not try the Watercress

Float, which is rich in vitamin A and iron, or the Celery Surprise, a fortifying tonic for mind and

body? If a dessert drink is more to your taste, the Berry Cream is a satisfying way to round off your

meal, and the Banana & Blueberry Smoothie will add some sparkle to your midday break.

berry

cream

how hard ✳ extremely easy
serves ✳ two
prep time ✳ 10 minutes
cooking time ✳ —

ingredients

350 ml/12 fl oz
orange juice
1 banana,
sliced and frozen

450 g/1 lb frozen
forest fruits
(such as blueberries,
raspberries
and blackberries)

to decorate

slices of fresh
strawberry

✳ Pour the orange juice into a food processor. Add the banana and half of the forest fruits and process until smooth.

✳ Add the remaining forest fruits and process until smooth. Pour the mixture into tall glasses and decorate the rims with slices of fresh strawberry. Add straws and serve.

banana & blueberry
smoothie

how hard ✳ extremely easy

serves ✳ two

prep time ✳ 10 minutes

cooking time ✳ —

ingredients

175 ml/6 fl oz
apple juice

125 ml/4 fl oz
natural yogurt

1 banana,
sliced and frozen

175 g/6 oz frozen
blueberries

to decorate

whole fresh
blueberries

✳ Pour the apple juice into a food processor. Add the yogurt and process until smooth.

✳ Add the banana and half of the blueberries and process well, then add the remaining blueberries and process until smooth. Pour the mixture into tall glasses and decorate with whole fresh blueberries. Add straws and serve.

banana & apple
booster

how hard ✳ extremely easy
serves ✳ two
prep time ✳ 15 minutes
cooking time ✳ —

ingredients

250 ml/9 fl oz
apple juice

½ tsp powdered
cinnamon

2 tsp grated
fresh root ginger
2 bananas,
sliced and frozen

to decorate

slices of fresh
banana
on cocktail sticks

✳ Pour the apple juice into a food processor. Add the cinnamon and ginger and process gently until combined.

✳ Add the bananas and process until smooth. Pour the mixture into tall glasses and decorate with slices of fresh banana on cocktail sticks. Serve at once.

strawberry & orange
smoothie

how hard ❋ extremely easy
serves ❋ two
prep time ❋ 15 minutes
cooking time ❋ —

ingredients

125 ml/4 fl oz
natural yogurt

175 ml/6 fl oz
strawberry yogurt

175 ml/6 fl oz
orange juice

175 g/6 oz frozen
strawberries

1 banana,
sliced and frozen

to decorate

slices of fresh orange

whole fresh
strawberries

❋ Pour the natural and strawberry yogurts into a food processor and process gently. Add the orange juice and process until combined.

❋ Add the strawberries and banana and process until smooth. Pour the mixture into tall glasses and decorate with slices of fresh orange and whole fresh strawberries. Add straws and serve.

celery

surprise

how hard ✳ very easy
serves ✳ two
prep time ✳ 15 minutes
cooking time ✳ —

ingredients

125 ml/4 fl oz
carrot juice

500 g/1 lb 2 oz
tomatoes,
skinned, deseeded and
roughly chopped

1 tbsp
lemon juice

4 celery sticks,
trimmed and sliced

4 spring onions,
trimmed and roughly chopped

25 g/1 oz
fresh parsley

25 g/1 oz
fresh mint

to garnish
2 **celery** sticks

✳ Put the carrot juice, tomatoes and lemon juice into a food processor and process gently until combined.

✳ Add the sliced celery along with the spring onions, parsley and mint and process until smooth. Pour the mixture into tall glasses and garnish with celery sticks. Serve at once.

curried
crush

how hard ✳ very easy
serves ✳ two
prep time ✳ 15 minutes
cooking time ✳ —

ingredients

250 ml/9 fl oz
carrot juice
4 tomatoes,
skinned, deseeded and
roughly chopped
1 tbsp
lemon juice
2 celery sticks,
trimmed and sliced
1 cos lettuce
1 garlic clove,
chopped
25 g/1 oz
fresh parsley
1 tsp
curry powder
6 ice cubes
125 ml/4 fl oz
water

to garnish

2 **celery** sticks

✳ Put the carrot juice, tomatoes, lemon juice and celery into a food processor and process gently until combined.

✳ Separate the lettuce leaves, then wash them and add them to the food processor along with the garlic, parsley, curry powder and ice cubes. Process until well combined, then pour in the water and process until smooth.

✳ Pour the mixture into tall glasses and garnish with celery sticks. Serve at once.

watercress
float

how hard ❋ extremely easy

serves ❋ two

prep time ❋ 10 minutes
+ 1 hour to chill

cooking time ❋ —

ingredients

500 ml/18 fl oz
carrot juice

25 g/1 oz
watercress

1 tbsp
lemon juice

to garnish

sprigs of fresh
watercress

❋ Pour the carrot juice into a food processor. Add the watercress and lemon juice and process until smooth. Transfer to a jug, cover with clingfilm and chill in the refrigerator for at least 1 hour, or until required.

❋ When the mixture is thoroughly chilled, pour into glasses and garnish with sprigs of fresh watercress. Serve at once.

summer & citrus fruit
punch

how hard ✳ extremely easy
serves ✳ two
prep time ✳ 10 minutes
cooking time ✳ —

ingredients

4 tbsp
orange juice

1 tbsp
lime juice

100 ml/3½ fl oz
sparkling water

350 g/12 oz frozen
summer fruits
(such as blueberries,
raspberries, blackberries
and strawberries)

4 ice cubes

to decorate

whole fresh
**raspberries,
blackcurrants**
and **blackberries**
on cocktail sticks

✳ Pour the orange juice, lime juice and sparkling water into

a food processor and process gently until combined.

✳ Add the summer fruits and ice cubes and process until a slushy

consistency has been reached.

✳ Pour the mixture into glasses, decorate with whole fresh

raspberries, blackcurrants and blackberries on cocktail sticks

and serve.

strawberry & peach
smoothie

how hard ✳ very easy

serves ✳ two

prep time ✳ 20 minutes

cooking time ✳ —

ingredients

175 ml/6 fl oz
milk

225 g/8 oz canned
peach slices,
drained

2 fresh apricots,
chopped

400 g/14 oz
fresh strawberries,
hulled and sliced

2 bananas,
sliced and frozen

to decorate

slices of fresh
strawberries

✳ Pour the milk into a food processor. Add the peach slices and process gently until combined. Add the apricots and process gently until combined.

✳ Add the strawberries and banana slices and process until smooth. Pour the mixture into glasses and decorate the rims with fresh strawberries. Serve at once.

fruit
rapture

how hard ✳ extremely easy

serves ✳ two

prep time ✳ 15 minutes

cooking time ✳ —

ingredients

100 ml/3½ fl oz
milk

125 ml/4 fl oz
peach yogurt

100 ml/3½ fl oz
orange juice

225 g/8 oz canned
peach slices,
drained

6 ice cubes

to decorate

strips of fresh
orange peel

✳ Pour the milk, yogurt and orange juice into a food processor and process gently until combined.

✳ Add the peach slices and ice cubes and process until smooth. Pour the mixture into glasses and decorate with strips of fresh orange peel. Add straws and serve.

traditional
lemonade

how hard ✳ very easy

serves ✳ two

prep time ✳ 15 minutes
+ 2½ hours to chill

cooking time ✳ 8–10 minutes

ingredients

150 ml/5 fl oz
water

6 tbsp
sugar

1 tsp grated
lemon rind

125 ml/4 fl oz
lemon juice

6 ice cubes

to decorate
wedge of lemon
granulated sugar
slices of fresh lemon

to serve
sparkling water

✳ Put the water, sugar and grated lemon rind into a small saucepan and bring to the boil, stirring constantly. Continue to boil, stirring, for 5 minutes.

✳ Remove from the heat and leave to cool to room temperature. Stir in the lemon juice, then transfer to a jug, cover with clingfilm and chill in the refrigerator for at least 2 hours.

✳ When the lemon mixture has almost finished chilling, take two glasses and rub the rims with a wedge of lemon, then dip them in granulated sugar to frost. Put the ice cubes into the glasses.

✳ Remove the lemon mixture from the refrigerator, pour it over the ice and top up with sparkling water. The ratio should be one part lemon mixture to three parts sparkling water. Stir well to mix, decorate with slices of fresh lemon and serve.

dinner desserts

You are in for a real treat with these dinner drinks, which are guaranteed to delight your family and friends. The Rich Chocolate Shake will enchant the chocolate lovers among you, and the Kiwi Dream will provide a refreshing and flavoursome finale to your meal. If you would like to add a twist to the after-dinner coffee theme, the Hazelnut & Coffee Sparkle will be a talking point, and the Pineapple Soda is a stunning drink to serve outside on warm evenings.

spicy banana
chill

how hard ✳ extremely easy

serves ✳ two

prep time ✳ 10 minutes

cooking time ✳ —

ingredients

300 ml/10 fl oz
milk

½ tsp
mixed spice

150 g/5½ oz
banana ice cream

2 bananas,
sliced and frozen

✳ Pour the milk into a food processor and add the mixed spice. Add half of the banana ice cream and process gently until combined, then add the remaining ice cream and process until well blended.

✳ When the mixture is well combined, add the bananas and process until smooth. Pour the mixture into tall glasses, add straws and serve at once.

banana & coffee
milkshake

how hard ✳ extremely easy
serves ✳ two
prep time ✳ 10 minutes
cooking time ✳ —

ingredients

300 ml/10 fl oz
milk

4 tbsp
instant coffee powder

150 g/5½ oz
vanilla ice cream

2 bananas,
sliced and frozen

✳ Pour the milk into a food processor, add the coffee powder and process gently until combined. Add half of the vanilla ice cream and process gently, then add the remaining ice cream and process until well combined.

✳ When the mixture is thoroughly blended, add the bananas and process until smooth. Pour the mixture into glasses and serve.

rich chocolate
shake

how hard ✳ extremely easy
serves ✳ two
prep time ✳ 10 minutes
cooking time ✳ —

ingredients

150 ml/5 fl oz
milk

2 tbsp
chocolate syrup

400 g/14 oz
chocolate ice cream

to decorate

grated chocolate

✳ Pour the milk and chocolate syrup into a food processor and process gently until combined.

✳ Add the chocolate ice cream and process until smooth. Pour the mixture into tall glasses and decorate by floating the grated chocolate. Serve at once.

maple & almond
milkshake

how hard ❄ extremely easy

serves ❄ two

prep time ❄ 15 minutes

cooking time ❄ —

ingredients

150 ml/5 fl oz
milk

2 tbsp
maple syrup

400 g/14 oz
vanilla ice cream

1 tbsp
almond essence

to decorate

chopped **almonds**

✳ Pour the milk and maple syrup into a food processor and process gently until combined.

✳ Add the ice cream and almond essence and process until smooth. Pour the mixture into glasses and decorate with the chopped almonds. Add straws and serve.

kiwi

dream

how hard ❊ extremely easy
serves ❊ two
prep time ❊ 15 minutes
cooking time ❊ —

ingredients

150 ml/5 fl oz
milk

juice of
2 limes

2 kiwi fruit,
chopped

1 tbsp
sugar

400 g/14 oz
vanilla ice cream

to decorate

slices of fresh
kiwi fruit

strips of fresh
lime peel

❊ Pour the milk and lime juice into a food processor and process gently until combined.

❊ Add the kiwi fruit and sugar and process gently, then add the ice cream and process until smooth. Pour the mixture into glasses and decorate with slices of fresh kiwi fruit and strips of fresh lime peel. Serve at once.

coffee
whip

how hard ✳ extremely easy
serves ✳ two
prep time ✳ 15 minutes
cooking time ✳ —

ingredients

200 ml/7 fl oz
milk

50 ml/2 fl oz
single cream

1 tbsp
brown sugar

2 tbsp
cocoa powder

1 tbsp
coffee syrup
or instant coffee powder

6 ice cubes

to serve
whipped **cream**
grated **chocolate**

✳ Put the milk, cream and sugar into a food processor and process gently until combined.

✳ Add the cocoa powder and coffee syrup or powder and process well, then add the ice cubes and process until smooth.

✳ Pour the mixture into glasses. Top with whipped cream, scatter over the grated chocolate and serve.

smooth iced
coffee

how hard ✳ very easy
serves ✳ two
prep time ✳ 15 minutes
+ 1¼ hours to chill
cooking time ✳ —

ingredients

400 ml/14 fl oz
water
2 tbsp
instant coffee granules
2 tbsp
brown sugar
6 ice cubes

to decorate
single **cream**
whole **coffee** beans

✳ Use the water and coffee granules to brew some hot coffee, then leave to cool to room temperature. Transfer to a jug, cover with clingfilm and chill in the refrigerator for at least 45 minutes.

✳ When the coffee has chilled, pour it into a food processor. Add the sugar and process until well combined. Add the ice cubes and process until smooth.

✳ Pour the mixture into glasses. Float single cream on the top, decorate with whole coffee beans and serve.

hazelnut & coffee

sparkle

how hard ✳ extremely easy
serves ✳ two
prep time ✳ 15 minutes
+ 1¼ hours to chill
cooking time ✳ —

ingredients

250 ml/9 fl oz
water

3 tbsp
instant coffee granules

125 ml/4 fl oz
sparkling water

1 tbsp
hazelnut syrup

2 tbsp
brown sugar

6 ice cubes

to decorate

slices of fresh **lime**
slices of fresh **lemon**

✳ Use the water and coffee granules to brew some hot coffee, then leave to cool to room temperature. Transfer to a jug, cover with clingfilm and chill in the refrigerator for at least 45 minutes.

✳ When the coffee has chilled, pour it into a food processor. Add the sparkling water, hazelnut syrup and sugar, and process well. Add the ice cubes and process until smooth.

✳ Pour the mixture into glasses, decorate the rims with slices of fresh lime and lemon and serve.

pineapple
soda

how hard ✳ easy
serves ✳ two
prep time ✳ 15–20 minutes
cooking time ✳ —

ingredients

175 ml/6 fl oz
pineapple juice

90 ml/3¼ fl oz
coconut milk

200 g/7 oz
vanilla ice cream

140 g/5 oz frozen
pineapple chunks

175 ml/6 fl oz
sparkling water

to serve

2 scooped-out
pineapple shells
(optional)

✳ Pour the pineapple juice and coconut milk into a food processor. Add the ice cream and process until smooth.

✳ Add the pineapple chunks and process well. Pour the mixture into scooped-out pineapple shells or tall glasses, until two-thirds full. Top up with sparkling water, add straws and serve.

orange & carrot

smoothie

how hard ✳ extremely easy

serves ✳ two

prep time ✳ 10 minutes

cooking time ✳ —

ingredients

175 ml/6 fl oz
carrot juice

175 ml/6 fl oz
orange juice

150 g/5½ oz
vanilla ice cream

6 ice cubes

to decorate

slices of fresh **orange**

strips of fresh
orange peel

✳ Pour the carrot juice and orange juice into a food processor and process gently until well combined. Add the ice cream and process until thoroughly blended.

✳ Add the ice cubes and process until smooth. Pour the mixture into glasses, decorate with slices of fresh orange and strips of fresh orange peel and serve.

evening cocktails

How could we finish this book without a tempting selection of cocktails? This section contains
some truly mouthwatering concoctions, which are perfect for entertaining or when you have a
few relaxing moments to yourself. When hosting a party, serve your guests the spectacular looking
Pineapple & Coconut Shake. For more intimate moments, the Cherry Kiss will bring a touch of
romance to any occasion, and the Rose Sunset will prove irresistible as the sun goes down.

pineapple & coconut
shake

how hard ✳ very easy
serves ✳ two
prep time ✳ 15 minutes
cooking time ✳ —

ingredients

350 ml/12 fl oz
pineapple juice

90 ml/3¼ fl oz
coconut milk

150 g/5½ oz
vanilla ice cream

140 g/5 oz frozen
pineapple chunks

to serve

2 scooped-out
coconut shells
(optional)

to decorate

2 tbsp grated fresh
coconut

✳ Pour the pineapple juice and coconut milk into a food processor. Add the ice cream and process until smooth.

✳ Add the pineapple chunks and process until smooth. Pour the mixture into scooped-out coconut shells, or tall glasses, and decorate with grated fresh coconut. Add straws and serve.

peach & pineapple
smoothie

how hard ✳ extremely easy
serves ✳ two
prep time ✳ 15 minutes
cooking time ✳ —

ingredients

125 ml/4 fl oz
pineapple juice

juice of
1 lemon

100 ml/3½ fl oz
water

3 tbsp
brown sugar

175 ml/6 fl oz
natural yogurt

1 peach,
cut into chunks and frozen

100 g/3½ oz frozen
pineapple chunks

to decorate

wedges of fresh
pineapple

✳ Pour the pineapple juice, lemon juice and water into a food processor. Add the sugar and yogurt and process until blended.

✳ Add the peach and pineapple chunks and process until smooth. Pour the mixture into glasses and decorate the rims with wedges of fresh pineapple. Serve at once.

caribbean vegan
cocktail

how hard ✳ extremely easy
serves ✳ two
prep time ✳ 15 minutes
cooking time ✳ —

ingredients

100 ml/3½ fl oz
coconut milk

200 ml/7 fl oz
soya milk

100 ml/3½ fl oz
pineapple juice

1 tbsp
brown sugar

1 ripe mango,
stoned and diced

2 tbsp grated
fresh coconut

140 g/5 oz frozen
pineapple chunks

1 banana,
sliced and frozen

to decorate

grated fresh **coconut**
wedges of fresh
pineapple

✳ Put the coconut milk, soya milk, pineapple juice and sugar into a food processor and process gently until combined. Add the diced mango to the food processor along with the grated coconut and process well.

✳ Add the pineapple chunks and banana and process until smooth. Pour the mixture into glasses, scatter over some grated fresh coconut and decorate the rims with wedges of fresh pineapple. Serve at once.

red

storm

how hard ❊ extremely easy

serves ❊ two

prep time ❊ 15 minutes

+ 30 minutes to chill

cooking time ❊ —

ingredients

500 ml/18 fl oz
tomato juice

dash of
Worcestershire sauce
1 small red chilli,
deseeded and chopped
1 spring onion,
trimmed and chopped
6 ice cubes

to garnish

2 long, thin red **chillies,**
cut into flowers (see method)

❊ To make the chilli flowers, use a sharp knife to make six cuts along each chilli. Place the point of the knife about 1 cm/½ inch from the stalk end and cut towards the tip. Put the chillies in a bowl of iced water and leave them for 25–30 minutes, until they have spread out into flower shapes.

❊ Put the tomato juice and Worcestershire sauce into a food processor and process gently until combined. Add the chopped chilli, spring onion and ice cubes and process until smooth.

❊ Pour the mixture into glasses and garnish with the chilli flowers. Add straws and serve.

peppermint
mocha

how hard ❉ extremely easy
serves ❉ two
prep time ❉ 15 minutes
cooking time ❉ —

ingredients

400 ml/14 fl oz
milk

200 ml/7 fl oz
coffee syrup

100 ml/3½ fl oz
peppermint syrup

1 tbsp chopped
fresh mint leaves

4 ice cubes

to decorate
grated chocolate
sprigs of fresh mint

❉ Pour the milk, coffee syrup and peppermint syrup into a food processor and process gently until combined.

❉ Add the mint and ice cubes and process until a slushy consistency has been reached.

❉ Pour the mixture into glasses. Scatter over the grated chocolate, decorate with sprigs of fresh mint and serve.

pineapple
crush

how hard ✳ extremely easy
serves ✳ two
prep time ✳ 10 minutes
cooking time ✳ —

ingredients

100 ml/3½ fl oz
pineapple juice

4 tbsp
orange juice

125 g/4 oz
galia melon,
cut into chunks

140 g/5 oz frozen
pineapple chunks

4 ice cubes

to decorate

slices of fresh
galia melon

slices of fresh **orange**

✳ Pour the pineapple juice and orange juice into a food

processor and process gently until combined.

✳ Add the melon, pineapple chunks and ice cubes and process

until a slushy consistency has been reached.

✳ Pour the mixture into glasses and decorate with slices of fresh

melon and orange. Serve at once.

hawaiian
shake

how hard ✳ very easy

serves ✳ two

prep time ✳ 15 minutes

cooking time ✳ —

ingredients

250 ml/9 fl oz
milk

50 ml/2 fl oz
coconut milk

150 g/5½ oz
vanilla ice cream

2 bananas,
sliced and frozen

200 g/7 oz canned
pineapple chunks,
drained

1 pawpaw,
deseeded and diced

to decorate

grated fresh coconut

wedges of fresh
pineapple

✳ Pour the milk and coconut milk into a food processor and process gently until combined. Add half of the ice cream and process gently, then add the remaining ice cream and process until smooth.

✳ Add the bananas and process well, then add the pineapple chunks and pawpaw and process until smooth. Pour the mixture into tall glasses, scatter over the grated coconut and decorate the rims with pineapple wedges. Serve at once.

rose

sunset

how hard ❉ very easy

serves ❉ two

prep time ❉ 15 minutes

cooking time ❉ —

ingredients

100 ml/3½ fl oz
natural yogurt

500 ml/18 fl oz
milk

1 tbsp
rose water

3 tbsp
honey

1 ripe mango,
stoned and diced

6 ice cubes

to decorate

edible **rose petals**
(optional)

❉ Pour the yogurt and milk into a food processor and process gently until combined.

❉ Add the rose water and honey and process until thoroughly blended, then add the mango along with the ice cubes and process until smooth. Pour the mixture into glasses, decorate with edible rose petals, if using, and serve.

cherry
kiss

how hard ✳ extremely easy

serves ✳ two

prep time ✳ 5 minutes

cooking time ✳ —

ingredients

8 ice cubes,
crushed

2 tbsp
cherry syrup

500 ml/18 fl oz
sparkling water

to decorate
maraschino cherries
on cocktail sticks

✳ Divide the crushed ice between two glasses and pour over the cherry syrup.

✳ Top up each glass with sparkling water. Decorate with the maraschino cherries on cocktail sticks and serve.

raspberry
cooler

how hard ✳ extremely easy
serves ✳ two
prep time ✳ 5 minutes
cooking time ✳ —

ingredients

8 ice cubes,
crushed

2 tbsp
raspberry syrup

500 ml/18 fl oz chilled
apple juice

to decorate

whole fresh
raspberries
and pieces of **apple**
on cocktail sticks

✴ Divide the crushed ice between two glasses and pour over the raspberry syrup.

✴ Top up each glass with chilled apple juice and stir well. Decorate with the whole fresh raspberries and pieces of apple on cocktail sticks and serve.

index